AF472156

==============

==============

==============oooooooooooooooo===========

Musings

(A)musing

(Un)amusing

(Quasi)amusing

By Lucette C. Bailliet

--------------oooooooooooooooooo============

POETRY

Also by Lucette C. Bailliet

Passing Flutterings I
Passing Flutterings II-Evanescence
Promenades I - On The Way
Promenades II-On The Other Side
Tree Change I - Our Place
Tree Change II- Entourage

THEATRE

Published as Alinor K. Austen

The Black Widow
La Veuve Noire (translation)
E.M., 2013
A Night To Remember

=============ooooooooooooooooo===========

=============== ==============

MUSINGS

ISBN: 978-1-4717-7125-5

=============ooooooooooooooooo===========

Poetry is when an emotion
has found its thought and
the thought has found words.

Robert Frost

==============ooooooooooooooooo============

Musings 2021

August-December

===============ooooooooooooooooo============

Table of Contents

==============oooooooooooooooo===========

August 2021

==============oooooooooooooooo============

1
Patched blue sky with black clouds
Glide over golden wattles
In late winter's day

2
White and red dusty tracks
Crossing with black and blue stony ones
Leading back Home
Where my heart is.

3
All is calm, peaceful
Everyone is asleep
On a grey winter morning
Cat, dog and man
Do not disturb

4
Failure, utter failure
Short they may be
Still have to be written
Two days and already failure!

==============ooooooooooooooooo============

5
The rattle of car keys
Heavenly promise
For the dog
Of travelling with the man
Happiness guaranteed!

6
Going from one emergency to the next
Daughter is fully vaccinated, yeasss!
Shepparton has 21 Covid cases
Schools closed. Bummer!

7
Mozart versus Bach
Genius versus hard yakka
The choice is easy
Not being a genius
It has to be hard yakka!

==============oooooooooooooooo============

8
Mockdown[1] town
Is the leading one in the country
Numbers are soaring
Bodies are piling
Doom is coming

9
This is the day
The day of the second jab
Here it goes!

10
Second jab in arm
I am a good citizen.
Prowling in the Forest
Walking on the wild side.

11
Open wide the door
Screeching cockatoos
Flying in wild sky

[1] Sydney

==============ooooooooooooooooo============

12
Walking in the Forest
Getting rid of cobwebs
And blues in the head

13
Curiouser and curiouser,
Second jab
No symptom, no pain,
AstraZeneca grows on me!

14
Windy day, blue sky
Walking in the Forest
Clearing the head

15
L …
Whatever inspiration it was
Went to never come back

16
Canola spread vies
Golden wattle globes
Spring covers its bases

==============ooooooooooooooooo============

17
Cows and sheep moving
On the chessboard of paddocks
What a game!

18
Almond trees and cockatoos
White bloom, white feathers
Which is the whiter?
Nature leverages her bets

19
Blogger be my guest
Entrance me, amuse me.
Beware, do not bore me
Commenter think first
Don't become a troll
No time for fiends.

20
Waking up, bleary eyes,
Hot shower, first comfort.
Running out of gas, cold shower,
First discomfort,
Thus the day starts.

=============oooooooooooooooo===========

21
Two males in this household
One too many
Who should be kicked out
The man or the dog?

22
Two females in this household
That's too many
One as useless as the other
The woman and the cat
Sleeping the day off

23
Blue sky, black clouds
Rolling over the horizon
When will this pandemic end?

24
The bar is rising
As the tally of dead bodies
You're still the first Gladys
What a competition!

===============ooooooooooooooooo============

25
Victoria wants to vaccinate
Supplies are short
Thanks to Scummo!

26
When numbers become names
It becomes personal
Covid is cruel

27
Black Angus,
White cockatoos,
All grazing lush paddocks
Spring is coming!

28
Only musos are welcome
To enter Silver Shakers
Exclusive Kirribilli bar

29
August in Covid lockdown
Cauliflower soup
Followed by orange cake
A night to remember

===============ooooooooooooooooo============

30
August hands over to Spring
White covered pear trees
Heaven for bees

31
August's imperial glory
A pain to go through
Mediocre weather

32
A gas leak fixed
Took us some time
But we're still alive
A day to celebrate!

==============oooooooooooooooooo============

September 2021

==============oooooooooooooooo============

1
Citrus glut not a problem
Lemon poppy seeds cake
Lemon pie, Orange cake
Orange and caramel crème
Who said it had to be boring?

2
Sun, glorious sun
Simple pleasure
Being outside
Despite Covid

3
Zero Covid policy dumped
Live with Covid is locked
Playing with lives

4
Propaganda for coming election
On reopening after Covid
Will life ever return to normal?

============--oooooooooooooooo===========

5
The infernal tally continues
New cases rise, Deaths too
Get vaccinated, they say
If it was so simple!

6
Stormy day,
Cold and windy,
Nice fire in the chimney,
Makes lockdown easier for today.

7
Obfuscation leads to confusion,
No worries we'll be right
Gambling with life

8
We're sorry for the families
A good thing about the dead
They no longer complain
About not being able
To get vaccinated

=============oooooooooooooooo===========

9
Dead Covid victim at home
Can't complain about
Lack of ICU hospital beds

10
So Father's Day, last Sunday
Happy hour on Skype
Scummo went back home
Missing his family so much

11
Scummo announcing a promise
Let's plan the end of violence
Against women in Australia
I say let's get some action man!

12
What a pleasure it is
Walking up the driveway
Lined with golden wattle

==============oooooooooooooooo============

13
Angel of fire
Must be uncomfortable
When overheating
These singed feathers
So keep cool.

14
Northern wind
Hot weather
Slow buzzing flies

15
For whom sounds the gong
Give me a song
I can hum along
Don't be too long

16
From today Glad is in hiding
She'll show up
Only for important reasons
Covid is no longer a sufficient one

17
Baron Trump's size is of import
Basketball is a good bet for him
A shame he isn't the right colour!

18
Gladys washing your hands
Doesn't wash with us
We've to thank you
For the lockdown

19
You're losing control
Gladys wilfully or not
You'll be remembered
By the lasting figures of the dead

20
As Pontus Pilate allegedly
Washed his hands off Jesus
So does Gladys of COVID-19 Delta
It's your problem bitch
That's why you got elected

=============oooooooooooooooooo============

21
The ever blithering evil ewe
Because of you
Millions are in lockdown

22
Not once, not twice but thrice
And you dare say
Learn to live with it!

23
The greed is strong with you
No wonder Murdock
Loves you!

24
Il est six heures
L'heure du cœur
Le soir tombe

25
Migrants versus country people
Hope for some, invasion for the others
The unmentioned crack in Australia

=============ooooooooooooooo============

===============   ===============

26
Hope, safety, adventures
Invasion, destruction, killings
Divided spirit and society

27
What changes a week may bring
To the season of Spring,
Its early blush gone
In donning a green gown

28
Gloom and doom
When heads of states
Play war games
In pandemic bloom

29
What has she learnt?
A better question would be
What has she found?
The answer is quite simple
Her voice!

=============oooooooooooooooo============

30
Hello dyslexia:
Canola and colza,
Cinnamon and cannelle,
Why can't my brain swap
From English to French
And vice-versa ?

31
Flies blown in with the Northern wind
Much too early mate
You don't care, do you?

32
Thumping noise?
Rattling noise rather
Small earthquake!

33
Shaken this morning
The forest awaits in silence
Save for the raucous kookaburra
Laughing at life as usual,
What a joker!

34
Let's toast the rogue nation
Aussie, Aussie, oi, oi, oi
Immigration, we decide who's in
Trade agreements, we tear them apart
Climate change, doesn't concerns us
Who cares? Not us, do you?

35
Covid is horrid
Scummo is worse

36
Empty MCG,
AFL grand finale
Drinking and carolling in WA

37
Sun setting
Choughs homing back
To the communal nest
Walking home in the dusk

38
Once again Gladys
Is in the forefront
Opening international travel, immediately!

==============oooooooooooooooo============

39
Covid is to be let free
To rip our society
In the name of the hallowed Economy
Oh Goodie! Can't wait!

40
Like a crab
I am currently home
Hiding from the world
Incommunicado, thank you!

41
11 am, rainy day
Still in bed hooray.

42
Spring shower
Unexpected and short
As it should be.

43
From the horizon
Black clouds rolling in
Never bursting
Life is a trail of betrayals.

==============ooooooooooooooooo============

==============   ==============

October 2021

==============oooooooooooooooo============

1
And the year spins out of control
Weather climate change is not worthy
Of headlines news:
Tornado in NSW yesterday
Will NRL finale play tomorrow?

2
Wow, Glad is out!
The golden girl bites the dust
Corrupt to the core she is
Denies it she does

3
With the rain brown-rot came
As well as corruption
She couldn't hide it any longer
Unglamorous she is now

4
October's a new month
A new beginning
When is SCUMMO's turn?

=============ooooooooooooooooo===========

5
So boring, another lockdown
Ever lasting Covid
You've exhausted your welcome
So piss off!

6
Latin be damned
Tomorrow is another day
It'd be cool to say that in Latin

7
And there goes my dream
Flat feet aren't allowed
In The Crazy Horse lineup!

8
A storm is coming in
No worries,
We're in lockdown

9
So John Bolinaro resigned too
He engrossed a staffer
I bet he is also corrupt
And Glad can't cover for him any longer.

==============ooooooooooooooooo============

10
A small short word
Two letters: if
Such power within though

11
If the weather holds
If the rain comes
If the fire season isn't on

12
If only Scummo
If…, If…, If…
Just think about it

13
We'll always remember you
1763 cases in Victoria
Because of you
We won't miss you Gladys

14
Warning: Toxic cocktail
Roman Catholic Church
Do not mix with education
Whatever the country

==============ooooooooooooooooo============

15
Vicious circle
Where there are children
There're pedophiles
And that's a fact

16
The Forest is filled
With the laughing ruckus of kookaburra
It's nice to know you're still there

17
You know spring has arrived
Not when the birds nest,
Not when the South Africa Cape weed bloom
But when you spot within minutes
Lizard and black red belly snake

18
Just a night work
Four hundred Roos in a paddock
One hundred and fifty five shot
Culling it's called

==============oooooooooooooooo============

19
Lockdown is off
Great! Can't have visitors though
What's the point?

20
Looks like game children play:
On, off, on, off, on, off, on, off,
On, off, on, off, on, off
It's going on for too long!
We are bored and tired

21
So NSW is celebrating Freedom
Victoria is mourning
Gladys' legacy is heavy

22
Something has to break
It's going to be ugly, I bet

23
Final goodbye, see you
On the other side of the pandemic
They say to the unvaccinated

=============ooooooooooooooooo===========

24
Your choice? Not vaccinated, lady.
You have a death wish, don't you?
We, the vaccinated, may be carriers

25
We might make it or not
You might not, it's your choice
See you on the other side
Of the pandemic

26
Two bottles of bubbly
Where did it all go?
Don't ask me

27
Pork barreling and gravy train
Go hand in hand
Gerrymandering and boys tie network too
Aussie corruption is as rampant, omnipresent,
And deadly as Covid

28
Murchison Scribbles
Scrap that this month,
Welcome to Murchison Tipples!

==============ooooooooooooooooo============

29
His heart[2] is no longer in place
Since his big fall down the stairs
Covid let it rip amongst us

30
Beady eyes, Greedy eyes
Evil eyes opened on the world

31
Lost in thoughts
Lost my way again
Misplaced in the Forest

32
With friends like you
Who need enemies?

33
Emotional and pecuniary blackmail
That is what it is, don't you know?
Proud of yourself, aren't you!

---

[2] Dan Andrews

=============oooooooooooooooo===========

34
Had a black swan moment
With the white Waratah
The old myths were right
It always existed but I didn't believe!

35
Lockdown World record : 265 days
Freedom on Thursday
How many are to die?

36
One death is a tragedy
Million deaths a statistic
Lesson taught by Covid

37
Do you have family?
My mother died a few years ago
My genitor is still alive
What else can I add?

38
The Forest is buzzing
So are the lavenders,
Honey ladies?

-------------=oooooooooooooooo===========

39
Fog is rolling in
Fog is rolling out
Swirling inside my head

40
A rose fragrance
Greets me in the kitchen
Good morning

41
To wake up daily
To a new bloom
Springtime joy

42
Blue columbines,
Red poppies
Lovely palette displayed
Bravo Dame Nature

43
Orange blossom and rose geranium
Poppies and columbines
Between beauty and scent
The garden is fragrant

=============oooooooooooooooo===========

44
Issue with getting up earlier
How to fill the longer day

45
I've heard the trees sing
Not the birds, the trees!

46
Oh dear, that's serious
The shelves to be empty
At Dan Murphy and BWS
Shortage or publicity stunt?

47
End clap, End game
Good friend, bad friend
Good titles,
Need to write now!

48
Too hot to work
Summer is coming
Hello hammock!

==============oooooooooooooooo===========

49
Summer is coming
Sundowners too
Hello spritzer and limoncello

50
You insult me, show me no respect.
The vomit from your message
Is an unending flow of ordure
Scream at your convenience,
I've blocked you
You don't deserve any answer
But I advise you
To change your medication

51
While one plays the bad friend,
Hysterical and out of control
To calm her nerves
The good friend
Loftily plays the injured party
What a pair!

==============ooooooooooooooooo============

52
What fools we are
To think the ground we walk is solid
Earthquakes and volcanos eruptions
The crust is cracking, melting, smoking
And still we bicker

53
Rumblings of war everywhere
Displays of new weapons capabilities
Walls virtual or not are going up
Pressure is mounting
Nationalism is rampant

54
Forget about climate change
Inaction will reign
Killing our neighbour
For a positive trade balance
How dare they?

55
Life is but
A trail of betrayals
Showing our frailties

===============oooooooooooooooo============

56
Did you know pork-barreling is legal?
Not so much corruption,
So affirms Gladys the Lady of delusions

57
Nocturnal sport
A spider, a large one hanging
Above my head in the night
Moving to the sofa
With quilt and pillows
Followed by cat.
Spider: ONE, Human and cat : ZERO

Colours of Spring

58
Colour in the garden: red
Red the bottle brush
Red the pig faces
Red the roses
Red the poppies

59
Colour in the garden : purple
Purple the lavenders
Purple the native Dianela
Purple the Sage
Purple the rosemary
Purple the iris

60
Colour in the garden : white
White the fragrant Orange blossom
White the enticing white rose
White the wintry forget me not
White the humble cheery daisy

=============ooooooooooooooooo============

61
Colour in the garden: yellow
Yellow the chrysanthemum flowering in spring
Yellow the gazanias so loved by the Roos
Yellow the South Africa cape weed

62
The garden is an array of colours
Somehow they never clash
Bringing it an urgent vibrancy
In the too rapid eluding spring

=============ooooooooooooooooo===========

63
Another week
And November signs in
How quickly October flew by

64
Another anniversary
Although it hurts me to call it so
The one celebrating your passing
Seventeen years ago.

65
Pipe smell
How curious
No one smokes here
Hallucinating?

66
Sunny corner
Stretching cat on the sofa
Sleepy happiness
Seizes the moment to relax

===============oooooooooooooooo============

67
So Gladys is going to spill the beans
She isn't going to take it for the team
The boys threw her under the bus
What a bitch she is, that's it for her

68
Her Majesty is ill
She still has to show up
For the climate change do
They shoot horses don't they?[3]

69
War is wagging under the pergola
Poppies corner versus daisies corner
Crimson red versus splashing white
Reproducing the war of the roses.

70
One has to wonder
Picking up a stick here or there
Putting them by the dam
Is the dog planning
To built a doghouse?

[3] movie title

============oooooooooooooooo===========

71
A dog's life
Jumping in thc car
Searching for stones
First thing in the morning
With the master
Pure bliss

72
A dog's life
Running with sticks
Jumping after sticks thrown in the dam
By the mistress
Digging in the muddy dam
On a Sunny day
Fabulous fun

73
A dog's life
Jumping in the trailer
To pickup rubbish bins
Barking madly at wild Roos
Favourite fun

=============oooooooooooooooo===========

74
In my birth country
Heroes were knights
In my adopted country
Heroes are footballers
It is hard to adapt.

75
LNP climate change plan
Keep going as we are
No change whatsoever
No surprise there, is there?

76
Drama in the making at the dam
Ducks in a flurry
Landing and taking off
In a moment
Breaking the peace
Galahs zooming madly
Between the gumtrees
Menacing shadow of an eagle
Sweeping over the dam.

=============ooooooooooooooooo===========

77
Pandemic impact on salutations
Not more " see you soon"
But in their place :"Take care, stay safe"

78
Prediction of stormy weather
Rolling in unstoppable
Like climate change.

79
Stormy weather outside
Mirrored by inner turmoil
Grinding of teeth
Bearing it all

80
And thus ends October
Freedom of movement
We're back to normal life
For how long?

81
Welcome to November
With delta plus on our shores!
A score more virulent than it's parent
Life is a wonder full of hidden surprises.

==============ooooooooooooooooo============

November 2021

==============oooooooooooooooooo============

1
Counting the days
Before she comes
Crossing fingers and toes

2
Rome, Glasgow
Looking to the future
Let's hop on planes
To reduce man influence
On climate change
Phonies, they are

3
Melbourne Cup
I wore my fascinator
He was down to his tradie's boxers!

4
Tickets bought
They're coming
Have to start cleaning!

5
He is coming
Fill the esky
Let's go fishing!

==============oooooooooooooooo==========

6
He will strip to his boxers
Mix some cocktails
Life is easy around him

7
Clear night, Clear sky
Am I brave enough
To touch the stars?

8
November is here
Prelude to the festive season
Will they make it here?

9
Paddock morphing into garden
House turning into a home
Five years in the making
Good things take time

10
Ibis has been spotted
New bird song filling the air
Bird refuge in the making?

==============ooooooooooooooooo============

11
Usual mess from wild ducks
Not on the concrete for once

12
Araignée du soir, espoir
Araignée du matin, chagrin
Je n'aime ni l'une ni l'autre.

13
Two countries,
Two cultures celebrations :
Melbourne cup
Beaujolais nouveau
And why not?

14
The question they ask is:
How fast do we need
To cut carbon emissions?
It's not how fast, it's now!

15
Act NOW
Not in 2030, not 2050
NOW!

==============oooooooooooooooo============

16
Can't put my teeth
Into November
I wonder why?
I can't be bothered

17
Walky call
Dog answers, disappears quickly
Spooked at its shadow
The cat appears shyly
She's a follower

17
Crickets sing
To the night coming
Cool and clear

18
Magpie warbles
"Good morning" at dawn
Magpie warbles
"Goodnight" at sunset
Thus the day is boxed in

=============ooooooooooooooooo===========

19
Offline panic
Not FOMO
Just unable to contact anyone

20
Some days aren't meant to be
Phone battery trying to escape
Replaced and caged again
But no wifi! Oh why!

21
An Angevin kind of day
Greyness guaranteed
Staying by the fire
Sole warm spot to be gotten

22
On the tv black screen
Fire flames reflecting
Meditation time

23
Poppies in the garden
Poppies for Remembrance Day
November makes sense Down Under

==============oooooooooooooooo============

24
No musings fluttering in my head
A boring rainy day
Drenched roses
Sagging bottlebrush

25
Trees are spirit, even stumps
Hail the Guardian,
Faithful and watchful
Hail the Senator
Who loves to harangue the Roos
When it rains.

26
COP 26 announcement
And Australia wins
Aussie OI OI
The Fossil award
Oi, oi ,….

27
First love betrayal
I wasn't even gone
He had already forgotten me
Didn't even turn up
To say goodbye!

=============oooooooooooooooo===========

28
The cloud mountains
Redefine the landscape
Framed by rain curtains

29
Weather stormy, how pretty
Silvery glistening gumtrees
Shivering under winds gusts

30
Cloud dragon mounted by Zeus
Checking on his week work
Crossing the skyline

31
Stormy, pretty but scary
Winds battling across the wide sky
Sweeping clouds, herding them
This way, that way
In an unknown strategy

32
Coal to be phased down
Not phased out
WTF COP26

==============oooooooooooooooo============

33
Friends or fiends
Announce you're unvaccinated
See the grain falling from the chaff

34
Four pads where we have two feet
Still keen to go walking
Loves dog and cat

35
Helium and hydrogen
Origin of stars
So we are full of gas?
Hot air I say!

36
Roasted by the Sun
No wonder we end up ashes

37
Not being Voltaire
I still respect your decisions
Although not agreeing with them
But I won't defend them.

==============ooooooooooooooooo============

38
What cause to choose?
Tackling Corruption,
International, domestic trade,
Environment ,Violence, Terrorism,
Wars, Refugees, Covid-19 vaccination
Rigged elections, pork barreling
Women inequalities and the list goes on.

39
One is spoiled to choose a cause today
You've chosen yours
I've chosen mine
They don't have to be the same
I don't have to agree with you
But l respect your choice.

40
Thus age makes itself known
Aches and pain, the order of the day
General malaise daily companion
Memory like hazy sepia
Colours one's day.

41
So you won't vaccinate
It's a question of principle
It's only a political ploy
Not only for big pharma
But to control masses so you say.
So is it a case of no jab, no play?

42
Gunshots in the night
And the culling starts again!
Blast be the man!

43
First they cut the trees
For the Forest regeneration
Now it's the Roos
To preserve biodiversity?
Allow me to doubt that.

44
I could lose myself
Truly spend hours
In that bookshelf of yours
Following the path
Of Children books leading
To a labyrinth of limited reality

45
What is more satisfying
Learning to recognise :
This is a duck,
That the sky is blue, and the sea green
How do certitudes bring comfort!

46
Time passes
Changes come and go
Murchison is dying

47
Loyal to her bosses
Secrets she kept
They removed her
Betrayed!

==============oooooooooooooooo==========

48
So difficult to organise a party
Everyone is twitching
Should I, shouldn't I go?

49
Don't ask me,
I'm sure I don't know
The colour of the sky
Everything is so murky
Lately

50
Secrets, more secrets
Resignation
Pub closing
Double brain tumour
I hate secrets in this little town!

51
When there are secrets
Community can't help
Open plunder of a town

=============ooooooooooooooooo===========

52
First and Last face to face meeting
Seven hours ranting and raving
Good to see people

53
Oh the beauty of silence
Deep and long
Alone with my thoughts

54
Cat running on the terrace
Chasing moon shadows
Stills in a moment
To bow in awe to the night

55
Picture of the Chat Noir cabaret
Comes to mind
Fusing time and minds

56
French saying
"At night every cat is grey"
No worries she is by day
But what a picture she made
Against the night sky

==============oooooooooooooooo============

57
She was grilled and roasted
Lasted for seven hours
She's still standing
Good on her

58
Time passes
Changes come and go
Forced on us
Willingly or not

59
They've never done
An honest workers day work
But on they don
Tradies' gear, boots and hats
To become more palatable
To voters night after night

60
Sorry to say
But his name should be
Kyle Rottenhouse!
Self-defence indeed

==============ooooooooooooooooo============

61
One ought to believe
That Oz's workers
Are all tradies!

62
Bogans are anti vaccination
But when cricket is announced
A hundred thousand blokes
Queued for a jab,
That's motivation
Cricket, indeed!

63
As the rain is coming
So are they
Let's get them

64
Vaccination alone is not sufficient
The fourth wave is rolling in
Lockdowns too are out
But masks are in
What a promise for us

==============oooooooooooooooo============

65
What a drag it is
To have to show " patte blanche"
Specially when government IT
Are incompatible

66
Refused entry to Bunnings
My VicServices Samsung
Not showing my vacc. certificate
I'll have to walk around with the IPad.

66
I know we're family but does he needs
To drop everything to his underpants?

67
His lack of clothing aside
He makes fabulous scrambles eggs
And high powered cocktails!

68
Fruit salad town
Do you really need
A new KFC franchise
Really?

=============ooooooooooooooooo===========

69
Macron and Omicron
Life can be deadly
Quarantine Morrison?

70
His trip highlights :
Playing guitar in the Forest
Fishing Murray Cod and Yellow Jacket

71
Delta and Omicron
Aside being Covid avatars of course
Develop a commonality of purpose
In their temporary hosts:
Frenzied traveling
Facilitating speedy spreading.

72
Take omicron for instance
South Africa - Sydney
Sydney - Melbourne
Melbourne - Sydney
The work of a day!

=============ooooooooooooooooo===========

73
Death latest advice:
Spread it around
Speed is of importance!

74
She's here, I tell you, she's here!
Come and salute her,
Come and salute our guest.
Have you seen it's latest avatar?
It's called Omicron
It comes under thirty-five strains
Beats Delta seventeen

75
You may disguise yourself
Under Greek outfits names
You'll be shortly running
Out of incarnations
For your catwalk parades.

76
Masks are back in fashion
Showing vaccination proof
Is a shopping obligation
Under refusal of entrance
For the harried masses.

==============ooooooooooooooooo============

77
Looks like double vaccination
Is not enough protection
Against Death latest incarnation

78
I tell you, as Perrottet said:
You have to learn to live with it!
To live or die with it!
A man of God this one.

79
Let them die, let them survive
God will recognise his own!
One can detect Opus Dei imprint.

80
Will we or won't we ?
Lockdown or not?
Merry holidays to you!

81
2022 seems to be another pattern
Built on the same base model
Than 2020 and 2021,
Not the roaring twenties
Of the last century. Damn it!

==============oooooooooooooooooo============

82
We're lucky really
We managed to have a break
To see friends and family
Before the latest onslaught

83
I understand now
The real meaning
Of those words:
Covid willing!

84
One may plan for sure
About one's future.
Better to dream though
Won't be disappointed then.

85
Sydney is under attack
Sydney is drowning
Under La Niña's onslaught.

=============ooooooooooooooooo============

86
Latest trend developing
No need to leave one's place
One can fish from
The upper windows
Of front water mansions

87
No longer wishing about
Million dollars water views
Better dry feet than wet ones

88
Don't know what
She'd been up to last night
But Dawn turned up
Grey and unkempt this morning
Took her ages to get her act together

89
Is a grey predawn
An oxymoron?

90
Breakfast at MIALLU
Brioche and black coffee
Kangaroo for company

=============oooooooooooooooo===========

91
Mornings at MIALLU
Cat on my left, purring
Dog on my right, licking
Patting them

92
Curtains drawn open
Sunny terrace
Trees bowing to Dawn

93
Hot day predicted
Extreme pollen levels
Poor Mim

94
Respect where respect is due
To the poets able to write
Seven poems a day

95
Proud of myself this month
For writing three poems a day
Until I remembered
The glorious seven

=============ooooooooooooooooo===========

96
November month of NaNoWriMo
Aims to write sixty thousand words
For beginning writers
Two thousand a day

97
And here I am
After four months
With four thousand words
Laughing (better than crying)
My ass off for my efforts

97
All things said
Omicron is the result
Of international mismanagement
WHO had warned us

98
We western countries have to share
The vaccination bounty around
Why? As if we didn't know
Now the result is here bitting our ass off
Karma is a bitch
When bothered to be

==============ooooooooooooooooo============

99
When will we ever learn ?
Omicron brings down
International borders
The Economy is going to suffer
Stuff it, I say.

100
All ready to go
Waiting for their modern slaves
Students, agricultural workers
With welcome signs
For the bosses wouldn't pay more
The local workers force
Here came omicron!

101
And real estate is roaring away
Debt is good they say
Buy now pay later they say
Something is sure to crash

=============oooooooooooooooo===========

102
Elections in May
Seven days in parliament
Yep you've read it
And they complain
Being a politician is so hard
Oh, come on, will you!

103
Summer came to visit today
Ready to move in tomorrow
Are you ready?

104
For the anecdotal side of it
Omicron was named
Skipping Nu and Xhi
To avoid misrepresentation

105
The gardener is proud
Of his daily work
Nature throws a spanner in it
Lovely plant flowering
He didn't plant nor nurtured
Way to keep him humble.

==============oooooooooooooooo============

December 2021

===============ooooooooooooooooo============

1
Hello Summer
Hoping you'll be kind to us
Bringing us a decent crop
Of tomatoes, zucchinis and aubergines

2
I understand you have
La Niña to contend with
Please do not roast us

3
Let her visit us
Water is needed
Down here

4
Vaccination diplomacy
China is to deliver Africa
One billion doses
While we dither

5
So Omicron was in Europe
Even before its African identification
Interesting isn't it
How racism spreads quickly

===============ooooooooooooooooo============

6
Speaking of racism
IGA's latest cashout policy
Speaks volumes
Press emergency button
As soon as Africans clients are identified
A second cashier will attend

7
Two cashiers to attend
Africans shopping
Or is it to tackle down
A possible Omicron attack?

8
Looking for real estate
Pure folly at the moment
Speeding frenzy feeding itself

9
She's right to set her future
Independently of his
Debt is good, he says
No way, I say.

=============ooooooooooooooooo===========

10
Echoes of Liberace's:
'Too much of a good thing
Is wonderful!

11
Basically he's a gambler
He's tripled his wealth
In twelve months

12
His soul is destroyed
He forgets to live
Even to love

13
I know I saw him at midnight
Almost crying on his screen
I felt he was
Going to commit suicide

14
Not once but twice
It broke my heart
So full of darkness was hc
Swirling around him
You might call it despair

=============ooooooooooooooooo===========

15
I tremble for her
If he goes she'll be on the street
So it's good she realised it
And plans ahead

16
Trying to read
Fly buzzing around my head
Summer is here,
Right on time!

17
Summer storm
First rain in weeks
Thank you summer

18
No wonder the internet
Was not working today
Thunderstorms on their way

19
Warnings kept coming
Fast and furious
All day long

==============ooooooooooooooooo===========

Circling around us
At last the storm
Is above us, hitting us

No need to water
The garden tomorrow

20 [4]
Modern percussion concert
Dog not impressed
Neither am I
But wait this is good

21
Violinist playing
 Not one note
Hail falling with drums

22
Silence plays a part
In modern music
So strange is our world

4 ANAM ALEXANDER MEAGHER Modern percussion end of year concert

==============oooooooooooooooo===========

22
Grey is the name of this piece
Glissement of the violin
Silence is grey

23
Clapping applause
The dog barks
Bringing a bit of joy

24
Going cross ears
I would say crossed arms
Can imagine children
Jumping, dancing, running

25
Red heart, blue vale (veil?)
Time and colour
Vibration rather than music
Hiding the melody
Maybe with reason
Overwhelming senses

=============oooooooooooooooo============

26
Not blue veil, blue steel indeed
Low vibrato brings anxiety
Anger, disquiet
Although the dog is snoring

27
Journey to Mocha
Inspired at an Indian restaurant
Nine stages

28
Just lost all my notes
On an electronic planner
I'm unhappy about it

29
Back to concert
This piece reminds me
The third volume of Yukio Mishima
When he travels to India
Engrossing and revolting
At the same time
Meditation bowls CD copycat

==============oooooooooooooooo============

30
Gifted percussionist he is
Needs others instruments
Unfortunately for him

31
Atlanta
Percussionist and pianist
Are battling to takeover
Ultimate dissociation

32
Like Covid-19
Morphing from delta to omicron
Bin chickens are evolving
From Ibis to Bush-Turkey .

33
I don't take to change
New look for my news source
New protocols and passwords

34
Why? More and more interferences
Big brother is inflecting dictatorial Diktats on us!
Hate this new trend by its universality

=============oooooooooooooooo===========

The rats are abandoning the ship

35
The Cunt is out of the building
At last, won't hear his blathering
Lying rat face any longer.

36
The rapist is out of the building too
That one was kicked out of the ship
Showing no remorse
Bitter to abandon the ship
Even if it's sinking (hopefully)

37
What a gleeful news to learn
The local National corrupt
Lying SOB representative is leaving
Because of him we lost DP Jones

38
The three above members
Had ambitions to the premiership
Politics taught them a lesson.

=============ooooooooooooooooo==========-

39
Summer is here
Bucket is in
Showering becomes Japanese

40
Honourable is their title
Dishonourable they showed
Themselves to be.

41
Heavy purring session
Good to see her trust
Five years in the making.

News you don't forget

42
New parenting trend
Text sent by mother after kid's arrest
For shooting dead four students
Using his Xmas pressie
I don't blame you,
But you need to learn
Not to get caught.

==============ooooooooooooooooo============

43
To get vaccination certificate
Man brings fake arm in Italy
Anti-Vax folly!

44
Xmas tree is up
Chimney trimmings are on
Switch on fairy lights
No sparks in my mind

45
Peaceful moment
In the reading nook
Soft lighting and music
Dog snoring softly
Daughter drawing in her diary
If only life could be that easy

46
At length, At the end
Eventually, finally,
When all is said and done
Don't you love English?

===============ooooooooooooooooo============

46
Demotic or common,vulgar
A new word, Oh dear!
Will I ever learn?

47
The thing with Xmas decorations
Too much of a good thing
Is wonderful and it's true
There's never enough
Of tawdry baubles to go around.

48
So it's difficult to know
When to stop
Isn't it?

49
How decadent
Peaches for breakfast
Early taste of Summer

50
She's in trouble
Having fell the ornaments
From the mantelpiece!

==============ooooooooooooooooo============

51
Her revenge for me
Not opening quickly enough
The door this morning?

52
Or just a dare to see if she could?
Or simple curiosity
For she's a cat.

53
Now I get the saying
" curiosity killed the cat"
How frustrating it is
To have to redo it!

54
Guêtres, mozzie net,
Gloves, hat and sunnies
The joys of gardening
In a Ozzie summer

55
How ironic it is really wishing friends
A Merry Xmas! and Happy New Year!
When 2022 looks so doomed already.

==============oooooooooooooooo============

56
New dietary rules:
No beef, less methane
No alcohol, no cramps
No chocolate, no guts problems
No milk, no more allergies

57
Squamous cells carcinoma
On the repeat
So drinking is a must
Bit late if truth be known
But savings in the making

58
Wishing you all
A Merry Christmas
Bit deflated I am
Readying to get
In the holidays spirit

59
Inviting people for luncheons
One is in hospital
The other is too busy
Catching up with relatives
So BLEH!

=============ooooooooooooooooo===========

60
I spent an afternoon
Perusing cooking books
For nothing

61
Have to find recipes
For mocktails
How fun it will be!

62
Shopping is not what
It used to be
A freezing experience
In Aldi stores
Doesn't let you muse
On your favourite staples

63
Given that the array
On display is rather limited
In the first place
It does not induce
A shopping therapy session

=============oooooooooooooooo===========

64
Bunnings having wiped out
Competition with its motto
“Prices are only the beginning”
Is letting the consumers down
Never seen such a dreary shop
Not a place to dream!

65
And then worse
Where is the Christmas spirit?
Not a tree, plastic or not, in sight
No Christmas ornaments either
In pandemic times
Life has to be celebrated
For goodness sake!

66
Everyone is shuffling around
Masked and quiet
Even the Muzak is absent
That is a plus really
Just saying!

=============oooooooooooooooo============

67
No bangers on the barbie
Well that's another plus
Just my take really

68
Back to Aldi,
What the hell is going on
Don't tell me
The containers of dental floss
Haven't made it to our shores
Slovenly distribution, me thinks.

69
Playing Irish music
On her tin whistle
He couldn't help but remark
'Never knew one could play
Using vacuum pipes!'

70
Oops! Some party it was
68 people became positive
All medics and nurses.

==============oooooooooooooooo===========

71
My compassion bag is flat empty
Not an ounce to be found
Not even a sparkle falling
When I turn it inside out

72
Totally depleted that is
What it is
I wonder how long
Will it take to replenish
Like a packet of Tim Tam?

73
Canceling a lesson for faulty internet
"No worries, Our internet
Will be down tomorrow too!"
Was the response.

74
You've got to love Aussies
Not much upset them
(maybe a problem)
Pragmatics they are.

=============ooooooooooooooooo===========

75
What an experience
Going shopping nowadays
The Australian way:
Sunnies, tick
Water bottle, tick
Mask, tick
Mobile, double tick
Bags, multi ticks
Cardigan, tick
That's it
Ready to hit the shops!
Oops, forgot the cards!
Blast, forgot the shopping list!

76
Recorder in hand, settling down to play
Dog and cat swiftly shy away
Not yet a performer by the audience.

77
So Glad is back
On the political agenda
According to Scummo
Integrity they can agree on
Missing in action on in both cases.

=============oooooooooooooooo===========

78
Strange day
I mistook the appointment time
Woke the complete household
On your face soldier!

79
How can one work in a closet
Three chairs and a computer
All masked of course
Get me out, give me air!

80
Ephemeral rainbow
Above the homestead
Splitting the ethereal sky

81
Shimmering rainbow
A shield from stormy weather
Barrier containing the worst
In the dusk of the day

82
Some have fame
Some have notoriety
Some don't mind.

=============oooooooooooooooo===========

83
Symmetry be damned
There's always the one out
To change the dynamics.

84
Dill, glorious herb
Or obnoxious weed
It all depends on you.

85
So glad to see you
Leaving the politics Gladys
May they be state or federal
Best news of the week
Bar Barnaby getting Covid.

86
Secrecy for a community organisation
Is a killer in action
Transparency is required!

87
A chair, a vice chair
A management committee
Wanking yourselves aren't you?

=============ooooooooooooooooo===========

88
There was never a meeting
Proposing members to be part
Of the Management Committee
No it was all kept in Camera

89
Well, well, well
There's always
An apt meme
For one's situation!

90
Cheap and neat
Or cheap and nasty
Our world staggers

91
Waste or not?
That's the question
Where profit is made

92
Rituals don't need
To be institutionalised
Make your own
To bring you joy and happiness!

==============ooooooooooooooooo============

93
The simplest tasks
Can be ritualised
Takc cooking for example
Bon appétit!

94
Brushing one's teeth
Brings your smile
To your world.

95
Officially enough Musings
A new book in the pipeline
Everyone applaud!

96
I wonder about bees
Sobriety is a moot word
Or so I have been told
Not when peaches are juicy ripe!

97
Open fructose bar
All you can sip
Alert for drunken bees

==============ooooooooooooooooo============

98
Sobriety might be
The daily grind
But even bees
Can brake rules

99
There's no such thing
As a free drink!
Warning sign
For drunken bees

100
Watch for hangover bees
Berroca everyone?
Go and sleep it off

101
He was in a hurry
To attend a party
For love doesn't tarry

102
Such a lovely tune
Stomping in my head
No need to drum it up
Staccato it ought to be

==============ooooooooooooooooo============

103
Two eggs in a nest
By the road side
No birdies yet

104
Two chicks nesting
Twice the size of the eggs
Already

105
New Caledonia has chosen
To stay a French colony
No need to visit then

106
When colonists are the majority
Independence is rejected
No surprise there

107
I dance in the wind
Arms spread wide
Dress flapping around me

===============ooooooooooooooooo============

108
Grief strips you raw
Grief is the price for love
Gone forever

109
She's anti-vaxxers
I'm for universal basic living wage
Never the twain 'll meet

110
Long time no see
Speaking of which
Where have the dragonflies gone?

111
Really!!!!!!
What was the point
Suffering lockdown after lockdown
If you decide to remove
Vaccination requirements ?

112
Consistency
Would be nice
You know!

=============oooooooooooooooo===========

113
Signs of dysfunctional governments
State regulations going one way
Federal mandates the other

114
Best wishes to Jenny Lister
You're sure to be missed
I don't envy the chosen one
Trying to fill your shoes!

115
Fire alarm screaming
Dog barking its head off
The quiche is sure to be crisp!

116
Christmas carols
Duets recorder practice
Dog snoring on the rug
Season oblige!

=============ooooooooooooooooo===========

117
Today's lesson
When the oven is on
An indispensable utensil
Is the humble umbrella
To switch off the fire alarm

118
Life is contrary
Be yourself today
Don't plan long term goals
Omicron time's coming first

119
At sunset
Sauntering in the Forest
Strident as a cricket

120
Such a shame
Money doesn't spread like Omicron
I would be a grateful recipient !

=============ooooooooooooooooo===========

121
Wait a minute
Spreading omicron
Like a grass fire in Summer
I wouldn't wish to be in Winter!

122
We all know about Xmas shopping
What about Xmas panic?
Shopping, testing and isolation

123
Does Santa know?
He needs to be fully vaccinated
To enter private households

124
Does Santa knows
He needs to be tested
For close contact?

125
Lonesome dragonfly
Chasing your own reflection
You're too beautiful to drown

==============ooooooooooooooooo============

126
Dust, heat, flies and mozzies
Came with the northern wind
All cleared up by the southern wind

127
Amongst the desert dust
The shimmering gumtrees
Are being shaken by the hot breeze
Bending this way, that way
Shading a branch or two
The Forest is a forbidden place today.

128
Don't know if it's a case
Of too much eating at Thanksgivings
Or kept too long in successive lockdowns
But the moon can barely scale the sky tonight

129
Fat and sweating
Brightly she glows
Filling in her duty
In the darkening sky

=============ooooooooooooooooo===========

130
Despite the dam turbid waters
The sky stays blue in its reflection
The trees shivering in the wind

131
You have to give them points
For trying that's true
Xmas carols cheers weren't convincing

132
Visitor on his way
This is a healing place
I feel in peace for the first time

133
We know he's a liar, cheat,
Alcoholic, drug addict, gambler
And gold-digger.
Still he is the groom
And his best man has to laud him.

134
How many marriages
Are entered in
Upon such dismal foundations?

==============oooooooooooooooooo============

135
It is a farce, a tragedy in the making
Receiving society's stamp of approval
What could go wrong?

136
How long before the cracks
Appear irreparable
And the lawyers move in?

137
Her nose in a book
Darling, I said
I drowned the dog
That got her attention

138
The stick was heavy and thick
I threw it into the dam
He dived to retrieve it
He got the bit between his jaws

139
He wouldn't let it go
Couldn't swim with it though
His head bobbing up less often

=============oooooooooooooooo===========

140
Dropped my hat, kept my shoes
Dived in, all dressed in
Swimming to retrieve him

141
Made it just in time
Got him by the skin of the neck
Took the damn stick away from him
Swam back to the bank

142
Let him go
Tried to walk off the dam
Slid back in the mud, fell to my four
Crawled out the water

143
The dog ran into the bushes
Terrorised, panicky
Although I called him, whistled
He wouldn't come to me

144
The breeze felt cold
After the warm turbid waters
I went home

=============ooooooooooooooooo===========

145
I wonder what would've happened
In winter ? Would I have jumped in?
But silly, he never swims in winter!

146
Christmas message to my chickens
Be merry and jolly
For in some households
You would be on the menu

147
Shouldn't dare Covid
Let it rip, the polies said
Hold my beer, it answered
And let it rip!

148
And the numbers increase daily,
Almost exponentially
What happens in countries with low vaccination ?

150
In the holy name of greed
Omicron is let to roam free
Dire Times to be

==============ooooooooooooooooo============

151
Love his new nickname
Domicron for the newest premier
What else can he expect!

152
Businesses are closing
Lockdown? No
Staff being pinged have to isolate
Oh the irony of it!

153
No honey moon period for him
Barely a month in
Already the butt of jokes
Poor Domicron ! Not!

154
Wind came in
Took away the nestlings
Lives wasted

=============oooooooooooooooo===========

155
This one can't eat seafood
That one is gluten allergic
This one is lactose intolerant
Chocolate is toxic to that other
Dinner planning is turning
Into a logistic and strategic exercise!

156
Iconic Aussie wine
Exporting to China
Despite trade embargo
"Californian" appears on the label
Above its brand name
WTF Penfolds! Media applauding !

157
Chasing the elusive booster
The federal govt says Moderna
Looks like it will be Pfizer

158
Snafu after Snafu
The tally increases
Let it rip they said

=============ooooooooooooooooo============

159
It must be dire
When Hunt is not
Daily on tv waffling about
What a good job
The feds are delivering

160
Midnight, murder hour
He came in my bedroom
In a disrobed state

161
The garlic to dry is rotting
And the smell is awful
Can't sleep!

162
Put it in the kitchen
Will see to that
In the morning

==============oooooooooooooooo============

163
No one realises
The existentialist problems
We experience on the homestead

164
Musing, (A)musing,
(Un)amusing,
(Quasi)amusing
One has to love English!

165
Stretched on the mat
She's doing yoga
Stretched on the wall
The spider holds positions

166
Have I just made a comparison
Between my daughter and a spider?
I bet I did!

167
She wishes to go to Melbourne
To visit her friends
I dread it, not because of her friends
But omicron!

=============ooooooooooooooooo===========

168
One happy person
Must be Gladys
How glad she ought to be
No longer her baby to nurse
She can retire in peace

169
Sign of the times
Instead of favours
For the wedding guests
He buys them RATS
In order to attend

170
Her panic attacks date
From princess Di funerals
If a princess can die
Then her parents too.

171
Any predictions for omicron year?
No need for them
The new year has already
Unsheathed her claws out!
It will do for the year of the Tiger.

==============ooooooooooooooooo============

172
I don't want her to go
I want to keep her safe
Here at our place
I know it's not possible

173
Let it rip
Last month of the year
Last day of the year
Who would have thought?

174
Such a year it was
And still I for one
I'm not looking forward
To tomorrow

175
Will the world be able to improve it?
For if Covid ever disappears
We still have climate change to tackle
Some challenge for the entitled generation

=============ooooooooooooooooo============

176
To hide its incompetence
This government keeps changing the rules
Of infectious contact,
It used to be mere seconds
Now five hours will do, thank you!

177
That way, restaurants
Retail, sporting events
Will stay open
No worries !

178
No more lockdowns
To stop the economy
New world coming
Business as usual

179
If you're sick, if you're old
That's your problem
How you deal, or not, with omicron!

=============ooooooooooooooooo============

180
You're in charge but as usual
You wash your hands
Passing the bucket
Of petty problems

181
He has ordered RATS
They'll arrive end of January
Small interesting detail
We are dying now!

182
Scummo doesn't give a rat
RATS [5] aren't his problem
It's the States responsibility
What a rat!

183
It's is favourite refrain
Not my business, mate
Well NEWS, for you, it is !

[5] RATS Rapid antigen test

=============oooooooooooooooo===========

184
It becomes our responsibility
To kick Scummo out
People let's get it right

185
And thus it ends
This sorry excuse of a year
With a booster shot

186
I should be grateful
To see its end
Lots of announcements
Nothing achieved

187
Dragging myself
From lockdown to lockdown
The year passed by.

===============ooooooooooooooooo============

188
It’s somewhat ironic
Kicking his wife out of his house
To live there with his mistress
Karma always polite
Returning a favour
His house has been sold
Without his agreement.
Karma in action!

189
It might be slow,
It might take some time,
It might come at the worst of times,
But Karma likes to settle accounts.

190
You may call it
Kismet, karma or fate
It will catch up with you
Do not worry about it.

=============ooooooooooooooooo===========

==============ooooooooooooooooo============

www.ingramcontent.com/pod-product-compliance
Ingram Content Group UK Ltd.
Pitfield, Milton Keynes, MK11 3LW, UK
UKHW040027200726
13854UKWH00001B/405